LORERS AND COLONIZATION™

HENRY HUDSON

Explorer of the Hudson River and Bay

HENRIETTA TOTH

ROSEN
PUBLISHING®
New York

For my niece Emi, who enjoys playing by the Hudson River

Published in 2017 by The Rosen Publishing Group, Inc.
29 East 21st Street, New York, NY 10010

First Edition

Library of Congress Cataloging-in-Publication Data

Names: Toth, Henrietta, author.
Title: Henry Hudson: Explorer of the Hudson River and Bay / Henrietta Toth.
Description: First edition. | New York : Rosen Publishing, 2017. | Series:
Spotlight on explorers and colonization | Includes bibliographical
references and index. | Identifiers: LCCN 2016023188 | ISBN 9781508172253 (library bound) | ISBN
9781508172222 (pbk.) | ISBN 9781508172239 (6-pack)
Subjects: LCSH: Hudson, Henry, –1611. | Explorers—America—Biography. | Explorers—Great
Britain—Biography. | America—Discovery and exploration—British. | Hudson River Valley (N.Y. and
N.J.)—Discovery and exploration.
Classification: LCC E129.H8 T68 2016 | DDC 910.92 [B]—dc23
LC record available at https://lccn.loc.gov/2016023188

Manufactured in China

CONTENTS

THE HUDSON WE KNOW

Henry Hudson was an explorer, navigator, and adventurer. He is remembered through the bodies of water named after him. The Hudson River is in New York State, and the Hudson Bay and Hudson Strait are in Canada. However, Hudson is probably best known for his tragic fate. His crew mutinied during his final voyage in 1611. They set him adrift and he was never found.

Hudson is often thought of as Dutch because he captained a Dutch ship on one voyage. He was actually English. He

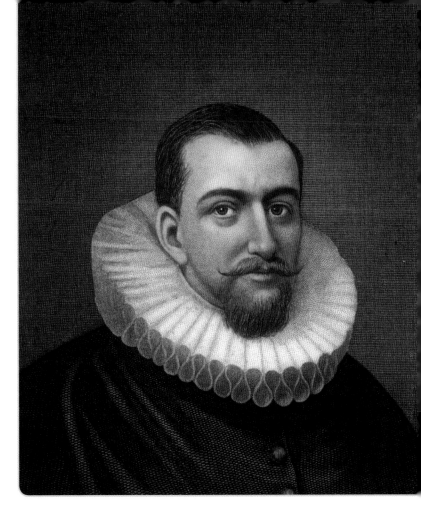

sought a northern passage to the East Indies by sailing through the Arctic. Hudson was convinced that such routes existed and that they were shorter than sailing around the tips of Africa or South America. If he found them they would open up new trade possibilities. He also hoped his discoveries would gain him fame and fortune. Though that never happened he is still considered a great explorer.

THE TRUTH ABOUT HUDSON

Henry Hudson was an English explorer and navigator who sailed for English and Dutch merchant companies. Companies like the Dutch East India Company sought him because he was a skilled and respected navigator. Hudson was also an innovative explorer. His expeditions led to the founding of the colony of New Netherland, which later became New York. In 1625, the village of New Amsterdam was established. This eventually became New York City. Hudson's exploration of the Hudson Bay led to European settlements and expansion in Canada.

Hudson sailed for the Dutch East India Company on his third voyage. Its shipyard and warehouse in Amsterdam are depicted in this 1725 engraving by Joseph Mulder.

Hudson was ambitious, like many mariners of his time. He also could be short-tempered and stubborn. Favoring some crewmen over others may have led to the mutiny on his final trip.

Hudson spent years trying to find a northern passage to the East Indies. He never succeeded. Like many explorers he was obsessed with finding this elusive route. Hudson thought his journeys had failed, even the one that sailed up the Hudson River.

HUDSON'S EARLY LIFE

Very little is known about Henry Hudson's youth. Hudson was likely born around 1565 about 20 miles northwest of London, England. He had three brothers: Christopher, Thomas, and John. Their grandfather may have been a trader who was also named Henry Hudson. Hudson probably went to sea as a cabin boy at about the age of sixteen. By the time of his first recorded voyage in 1607 he was an experienced captain.

In the early 1590s, Hudson married a woman named Katherine. The Hudsons' sons

were Richard, John, and Oliver. John sailed on all of his father's voyages. He served as ship's boy on Hudson's last voyage. John was set adrift with his father and a few other sailors when the crew mutinied.

No one knows what Hudson looked like. A Dutch mapmaker may have engraved a picture of him, but it is lost. A portrait painted in the nineteenth century shows how he might have looked, though.

LIFE BEFORE THE VOYAGES

Henry Hudson entered the pages of history in 1607 as captain of his first voyage. It is believed that Hudson sailed on English vessels before commanding his own voyages. These trips may be how Hudson learned navigation skills. He may have sailed on trading routes to the Mediterranean and Africa. When John Davis went to the Arctic in 1587 Hudson may have gone along. In 1588, he might have even served on an English ship that fought the Spanish Armada.

Hudson probably worked for the Muscovy Company in London. His family

Hudson charted his routes using a compass and other early navigational instruments.

owned shares in the company, which traded goods between England and Russia. Hudson was influenced by the voyages of Christopher Columbus and Vasco da Gama. They had both sought new routes to the East Indies. Hudson may have helped convince the Muscovy Company to fund his expedition in search of a northern passage through the Arctic.

HUDSON AS MARITIME NAVIGATOR

It is not known where Henry Hudson gained his nautical training, but it is believed that he was well educated. He had skills in astronomy, cartography, and mathematics. Like most navigators of his time, Hudson paid careful attention to detail. Hudson could tell if his ship was sailing into treacherous, icy water. How? The color of the sea would change from green to blue-black. Other mariners followed Hudson's findings when sailing in the Arctic region. They did this because Hudson was one of the few explorers to bring his ships safely back home.

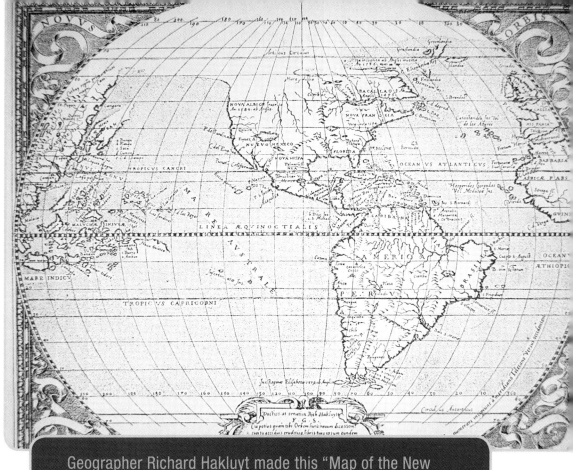

Geographer Richard Hakluyt made this "Map of the New World" in 1587. It shows North and South America as they were thought to be at the time.

Hudson was a talented navigator, but he was not a very good leader. On all four of his voyages his crew was unhappy. They feared traveling in uncharted and frigid waters with dwindling food supplies.

Hudson studied the charts and maps of English geographer Richard Hakluyt. Hakluyt may have helped him get command of his first voyage in 1607.

THE NORTHERN PASSAGES

Henry Hudson lived during the golden age of exploration. This was the start of colonization and globalization. All of Europe was obsessed with sea exploration and finding northern trade routes. Two possible passages, if they existed, would shorten the trip between Europe and the East Indies. One was a northwest passage through North America. The other was a northeast passage across the North Pole.

Crushing ice, incomplete maps of the world, and bodies of water yet to be discovered stood in the way. A few

Icebergs, like these in Disko Bay in Greenland, prevented early explorers from finding new routes to the East Indies.

navigators before Hudson and several after him tried. In 1878, Swedish explorer Adolf Erik Nordenskiöld traveled through the Northeast Passage. The Northwest Passage was discovered in 1905 by Norwegian explorer Roald Amundsen. He found it by crossing the Bering Strait across the top of North America into the Pacific Ocean. The passages are only free from ice for a short time each year.

THE FIRST VOYAGE, 1607

Henry Hudson set sail as commander of his first voyage on April 23, 1607. The *Hopewell*, an English bark, left London with a crew of ten men. Hudson's teenage son, John, was included. Hudson set an eastward course that would take him into the Arctic region across the North Pole. Bad weather slowed the trip from the start.

At the end of May the crew noticed that the ship's compass was defective. They saw this as a bad omen and worried that the voyage was cursed. Hudson barely calmed

Ice floes posed a constant danger on three of Hudson's explorations of the northern passages.

the men and prevented a mutiny. The threat of mutiny from frightened sailors plagued Hudson on all four of his voyages.

By June 13, the *Hopewell* arrived along the coast of Greenland. From there, it sailed north. Hudson made maps of the coastline and explored nearby islands.

At the north end of Greenland, Hudson was forced to sail northeast to avoid ice floes and freezing, foggy weather. Extreme cold and large choppy ice surrounded the *Hopewell*. In late June, it sailed 600 miles north of Norway to the Spitsbergen Islands.

In mid-July the *Hopewell* was about 750 miles north of the Arctic Circle. Hudson wrote about the midnight sun in his journal. In a place called Whale Bay the crew spotted many whales. The sailors took this as another bad omen. It turned out to be a good omen for English whalers, though. After Hudson reported his sightings of the large mammals the whaling industry took off.

By late July the *Hopewell* came within 577 miles of the North Pole before ice blocked their way. Hudson managed to save the ship from colliding with an iceberg. Winter began to settle in so Hudson sailed south for home. He arrived in London on September 15.

THE SECOND VOYAGE, 1608

The Muscovy Company wanted Henry Hudson's next voyage to be a whale hunt. Hudson was more interested in finding a northern passage to the East Indies. Despite Hudson's unsuccessful first expedition, he talked the Muscovy Company into funding another voyage. On April 25, 1608, Hudson left London aboard the *Hopewell*. Extra planks had been added since his last voyage to strengthen the hull against ice. The crew of fifteen again included Hudson's son John. The *Hopewell* followed a north-east course. Also on board was master

Hudson had a long association with the Muscovy Company. This seal of the company was found in London in the sixteenth century.

seaman Robert Juet. Hudson noted that Juet had a mean temper.

The *Hopewell* headed for Norway. By the end of May, the crew had reached the northern part of the country. They ran into foul weather on the Barents Sea. Ice and fog threatened the safety of the ship and crew. Luckily, Hudson's skill as a navigator brought them safely through. Next, Hudson sailed northeast of Russia through the Arctic Ocean in search of the Northeast Passage. In mid June, two sailors reported seeing a mermaid in the water!

On June 27, the *Hopewell* reached a long island called Novaya Zemlya. It sat in the Arctic Ocean off northern Russia. Thick ice once again blocked the ship's path and forced the crew to turn back. On July 5, Hudson's crew thought he was heading for England. Secretly, though, he had charted a course for North America and the Northwest Passage. By August 7, the crew realized that

Large glaciers cover the Arctic island of Novaya Zemlya. Hudson reached this island on his second voyage.

the *Hopewell* was not headed for England. They threatened mutiny if Hudson did not sail home.

In late August, the *Hopewell* arrived in London. Hudson could not convince the Muscovy Company to support more expeditions in search of a northern route to the East Indies.

THE THIRD VOYAGE, 1609

The Dutch East India Company hired Henry Hudson to find a shorter sea route to the spice trade of the East Indies. Hudson's third voyage is famous for his exploration of the North American coast. Hudson set sail from Amsterdam, Holland, on April 6, 1609, in the Dutch ship *Half Moon*. The crew of about twenty Dutch and English sailors did not speak each other's language, which made it hard to communicate. On board again were Hudson's son John and Robert Juet.

Hudson agreed to search only for the Northeast Passage. He headed for the

A replica of the *Half Moon* sailed up the Hudson River in 2009 during the four hundredth anniversary celebration of Hudson's discovery of the waterway.

island of Novaya Zemlya in the Arctic Ocean. By late May severe weather near northern Norway forced Hudson to turn back. He resisted returning to the Netherlands, though. Instead, he talked his crew into sailing west across the Atlantic Ocean. There, he meant to search for the Northwest Passage. By July 8, the ship reached Newfoundland. It sailed down the coast of North America as far as Virginia.

The crew then turned north and sailed past Delaware Bay and along the New Jersey coast.

On September 11, the *Half Moon* entered present-day New York Harbor. About thirty canoes carrying native people met the ship. The crew did not trust the natives but traded

with them for food. The *Half Moon* continued upriver, coming to the widest point at what later became Tarrytown, New York, on September 14. The brackish water made Hudson think he might have found the Northwest Passage. The ship sailed further north to present-day Albany. There, the decreasing tides and clearer water made Hudson realize he had failed again.

The *Half Moon* headed back downriver. Near today's Peekskill the crew traded with Native Americans for food. A sailor shot and killed a native man for stealing from the ship. The next day about one hundred Native Americans attacked the *Half Moon*. On October 4, the ship set sail for Europe. It arrived in England on November 7. There, Hudson was arrested for sailing for a foreign country.

THE FOURTH VOYAGE, 1610–1611

Despite his failure to find a northern route, Henry Hudson found funding for another voyage. His final trip took place aboard a larger ship with a larger crew. Hudson set sail on April 17, 1610, from London aboard the *Discovery*. The crew of twenty men again included his son John and Robert Juet. The ship carried enough supplies for eight months.

On reaching northern Canada, the *Discovery* sailed northwest from the Atlantic Ocean into Hudson Strait. Violent water and massive ice terrified the crew. They nearly

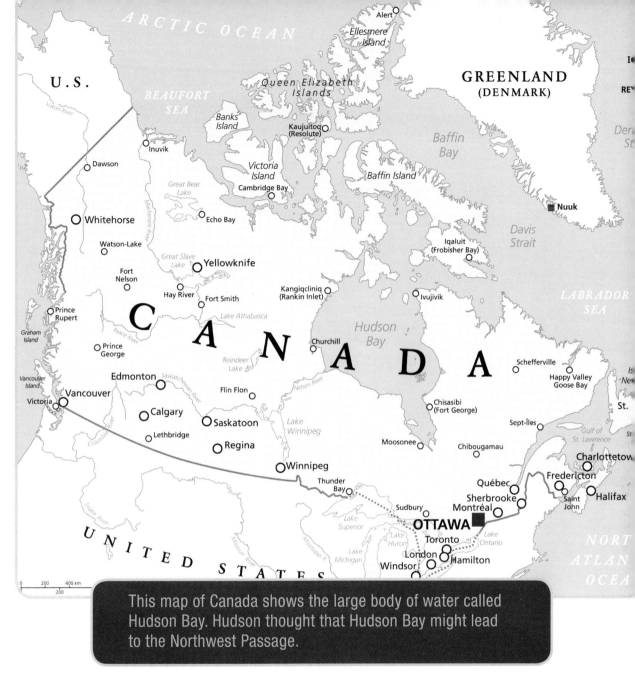

This map of Canada shows the large body of water called Hudson Bay. Hudson thought that Hudson Bay might lead to the Northwest Passage.

caused a mutiny. Hudson convinced his men to sail on. By August 2, the *Discovery* turned southwest and entered a large body of water we know today as Hudson Bay.

Hudson kept sailing south, thinking he had found the Northwest Passage.

By October 31, Hudson realized he had reached a dead end. The ship had arrived in the southern portion of James Bay. There, the water was too shallow. Hudson did not seem to know which direction to try next. Juet confronted him in front of an angry crew and Hudson demoted him. The *Discovery* was unable to sail for England before winter set in. Now the crew had few supplies to live on until the winter ice broke in mid June. Hudson wanted to continue searching for the Northwest Passage. His crew was fed up and wanted to go home. On June 22, Juet and the men mutinied. The crew set Hudson, his son John, and six other sick and loyal sailors adrift in a shallop in Hudson Bay. They were never seen again.

The remaining crew set sail for England. Before heading across the Atlantic Ocean they stopped at Digges Island for water and food. Inuit natives killed the leaders of the mutiny, except for Juet. He died of starvation about one week before reaching home. Only a handful of men returned to England and were arrested for mutiny.

MUTINY OR MURDER?

Henry Hudson's last voyage in search of a northern passage ended in mutiny. On all four of Hudson's voyages his crew was close to mutiny. This time Hudson may have pushed them over the edge. The crew was starving and Hudson did not ration food properly. He secretly gave more food to his favorite crewmen. He also demoted Robert Juet, the *Discovery*'s log keeper. This made Juet and the crew angry. Another crewman named Henry Greene may have led the mutiny.

Hudson, his son John, the ship's carpenter, and six sailors suffering from

Dense hardtack and dry cheese were common foods aboard a ship. Hardtack was a biscuit made of flour and water that lasted a long time.

scurvy were forced into a shallop. The *Discovery* sailed away, leaving the shallop far behind. How long could Hudson and his abandoned men survive in a small boat in harsh conditions? They did not have provisions, such as food and warm clothes. Did the native people help them or kill them? There is a theory that Henry Hudson and his men lived among the local native people.

Some scholars think that Hudson was murdered during the violent mutiny. If Hudson was cast into the shallop alive, the mutiny likely led to his death.

Less than ten sailors made it back to England aboard the *Discovery*. The mutiny was investigated. Most people expected the sailors to hang, but the surviving crew was put on trial six years later and acquitted (completely discharged). They blamed the mutineers who were killed in the Inuit attack on the way home. They also claimed to know how to find the Northwest Passage based on the *Discovery*'s voyage.

Three years after the mutiny, a search ship was sent after Hudson and his abandoned crew. No trace of them was ever found. Later explorers came upon the remains of a wooden shelter on Danby Island in James Bay, Canada. It could have been built by the *Discovery*'s carpenter.

HUDSON AND THE NATIVE AMERICANS

On Henry Hudson's third voyage to the New World, he met with native groups several times. Hudson and the crew of the *Half Moon* distrusted the native people. Hudson described them as appearing friendly, but he also called them thieves who carried off whatever they wanted. The Native Americans described the *Half Moon* as "a large house of various colors." They also said that Hudson wore a "red coat all glittering with lace."

Hudson's crew traded with the Native Americans. They exchanged knives and

Hudson greets Native Americans in *The Discovery of the Hudson,* painted by Albert Bierstadt in 1874. This scene takes place farther up the river in the Hudson River valley.

hatchets for animal furs and food like bread, corn, and oysters. Hudson's men also got the natives drunk so that they would part with more furs.

Some meetings with native groups led to violence, especially along the lower Hudson River. Along the upper Hudson River, the *Half Moon* crew met the Mohegan tribe whom they called "loving people."

HUDSON'S LEGACY

Henry Hudson's name is used for more waterways than that of any other explorer. However, there is more to Hudson's legacy. His four voyages were unsuccessful in finding a northern passage. Still, he sailed farther north than any other navigator until 1773. He traveled in previously uncharted waters to distant and new lands. His expeditions contributed to the knowledge of the Arctic regions and put them on the world map.

Hudson discovered what soon became Dutch New York. The Wall Street district of

This Hudson River waterfront in New Jersey is seen from New York City. Both river banks have been greatly developed since Hudson sailed up the waterway in 1609.

New York later became the financial capital of the world. He discovered New York Harbor. It developed into an important shipping and commercial trading center. He also explored the Hudson River, which grew into a major shipping lane.

Hudson was among the first Europeans to meet and trade with native tribes along the Hudson River. His reaction to them influenced how later colonists would treat the native people.

CELEBRATING HUDSON

In 1909 the Hudson-Fulton Celebration took place. It honored the three hundredth anniversary of Henry Hudson's voyage up the Hudson River. (It also celebrated the one hundredth anniversary of Robert Fulton's first successful commercial venture in a paddle steamer.) The celebration was held again in 2009 for the four hundredth anniversary of Hudson's discovery of the river. Stamps were issued for the 1909 celebration. Britain honored Hudson on stamps in 1972, as did Canada in 1986.

The Henry Hudson Monument is a bronze statue of the first European to explore the river that now bears his name.

Hudson's name is used for bodies of water like the Hudson River, Hudson Bay, and Hudson Strait. Hudson County in New Jersey and the town of Hudson in upstate New York are named for the explorer. A statue of him was erected in 1939 in Henry Hudson Park in the Bronx, New York. Standing on a one hundred-foot column, Hudson appears to be looking out over the Hudson River.

Hudson and his abandoned crew even appear as ghostly characters in Washington Irving's famous tale "Rip Van Winkle."

GLOSSARY

Arctic The region around the North Pole.

astronomy The study of the stars, planets, and sun.

bark A ship that has three or more masts with specific types of sails.

cartography The design and production of maps.

colonize To form a new settlement that has ties to a parent country.

compass An instrument used to find directions.

East Indies The name for a group of southeast Asian countries, including Indonesia and India.

globalize To create a worldwide influence.

hull The watertight bottom and sides of a ship.

ice floe A large pack of floating ice.

Inuit A group of native peoples who live in northern North America.

legacy Something that is handed down from the past.

mariner A seaman or sailor.

midnight sun The sun when it is seen at midnight in the Arctic.

mutiny A rebellion by sailors against the captain and officers of a ship.

navigator A person who guides a ship through water.

scurvy A disease caused by lack of Vitamin C.

shallop A small boat that can be sailed or rowed in shallow water.

ship's boy A young boy who serves on board a ship by waiting on its crew.

Hudson River Maritime Museum
50 Rondout Landing
Kingston, NY 12401
(845) 338-0071
Website: http://www.hrmm.org
The maritime and Dutch history of the Hudson River
is told through art displays and even boat building
classes. An exhibit on Henry Hudson and his
exploration of the Hudson River includes a replica
of the rear cabin of the *Half Moon.*

The Mariners' Museum and Park
100 Museum Drive
Newport News, VA 23606
(757) 596-2222
Website: http://www.marinersmuseum.org
The Age of Exploration Gallery at the museum
presents the development of ocean exploration
from the fifteenth through the eighteenth centuries.
Ship models, navigational tools, and other artifacts
show how early explorers discovered and mapped
new lands.

New Netherland Institute
P.O. Box 2536
Empire State Plaza
Albany, NY 12220

(518) 486-4815
Website: http://www.newnetherlandinstitute.org
The institute celebrates, promotes, and researches
    America's Dutch roots with news, events, and
    programs.

Westfries Museum
Roode Steen 1
1621 CV Hoorn,
Netherlands
+31 229 28 00 22
Website: http://www.westfriesmuseum.info
A 1989 replica of the *Half Moon* can be toured at
    this regional art and history museum in northern
    Holland. Visitors will be surprised at the small ship
    Henry Hudson sailed across the Atlantic Ocean.

Websites

Because of the changing nature of internet links,
Rosen Publishing has developed an online list of
websites related to the subject of this book. This site
is updated regularly. Please use this link to access
this list:

http://www.rosenlinks.com/SEC/hudson

Cooke, Tim. *Explore with Henry Hudson* (Travel with the Great Explorers). New York, NY: Crabtree Publishing Company, 2014.

Dalton, Anthony. *Henry Hudson: Doomed Navigator and Explorer.* Victoria, BC: Heritage House Publishing, 2014.

Goodman, Edward C., ed. *The Hudson River Valley Reader.* Kennebunkport, ME: Cider Mill Press, 2012.

Goodman, Joan Elizabeth. *Beyond the Sea of Ice: The Voyages of Henry Hudson.* New York, NY: Mikaya Press, 2015.

Gould, Jane. *Henry Hudson* (Jr. Graphic Famous Explorers). New York, NY: Powerkids Press, 2013.

Lourie, Peter. *Hudson River: An Adventure from the Mountains to the Sea.* Addison, VT: Snake Mountain Press, 2014.

Mooney, Carla. *Explorers of the New World: Discover the Golden Age of Exploration With 22 Projects.* White River Junction, VT: Nomad Press, 2011.

Talbott, Hudson. *River of Dreams: The Story of the Hudson River.* New York, NY: G.P. Putnam's Sons, 2009.

Weaver, Janice. *Hudson.* Toronto, ON: Tundra Books, 2011.

Young, Jeff C. *Henry Hudson: Discoverer of the Hudson River* (Great Explorers of the World). Berkeley Heights, NJ: Enslow Publishing, 2009.

BIBLIOGRAPHY

Cavendish, Richard. "Henry Hudson Sails Into Hudson Bay." History Today, August 8, 2010. http://www .historytoday.com/richard-cavendish/henry-hudson -sails-hudson-bay.

Holmes, Charlie. "What Really Happened to Henry Hudson." *Register Star*, January 2016. http://www .registerstar.com/news/article_00c30e52-b562-11e5 -9a5b-93b4e8a17122.html.

Hunter, Douglas. *Half Moon: Henry Hudson and the Voyage that Redrew the Map of the New World.* New York, NY: Bloomsbury Press, 2009.

La Manna, Bernadette. "Charting His Own Course: Henry Hudson's Remarkable Voyages." *Conservationist*, August 2009. http://www.dec .ny.gov/pubs/conservationist.html.

Mancall, Peter C. *Fatal Journey: The Final Expedition of Henry Hudson.* New York: Basic Books, 2010.

Mariner's Museum. "Henry Hudson." Exploration Through the Ages. Retrieved April 15, 2016. http://ageofex .marinersmuseum.org/index.php?type=explorer&id=15.

Roberts, Sam. "Henry Hudson's View of New York: When Trees Tipped the Sky." *New York Times*, January 24, 2009. http://www.nytimes.com/2009/01/25/ nyregion/25manhattan.html?_r=0.

Rothstein, Edward. "Voyaging Up the Hudson to Rediscover the Dutch." *New York Times*, May 8, 2009. http://www.nytimes.com/2009/05/09/arts/ design/09huds.html.

INDEX

About the Author

Henrietta Toth is a writer and editor with nearly twenty years' experience in academic publishing. She enjoys reading and writing about early world history as a career as well as a hobby. She has always lived near the Hudson River.

Photo Credits